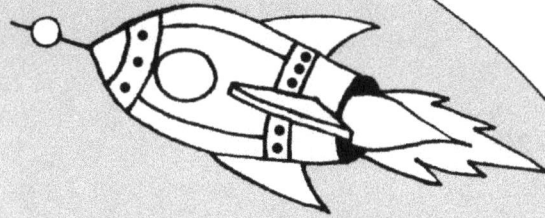

Preschool Fun Learning My ABC 123

Johnson, Kay D
Preschool Fun Learning My ABC 123
ISBN 978-1-989382-02-8 (pbk)

a a a

b b b

c c c

d d d

e e e

f f f

g g g

h h h

i i i i

j j j j

k k k

l l l l

m m m

n n n

o o o

p p p

q q q

r r r

S S S

t t t

u u u

v v v

w w w

x x x

y y y

z z z

A A A

B B B

C C C

D D D

E E E

F F F

G G G

H H H

I I I

J J J J

K K K K

L L L L

M M M M

N N N N

O O O

P P P

Q Q Q

R R R

S S S

T T T

U U U

V V V

W W W

X X X

Y Y Y

Z Z Z

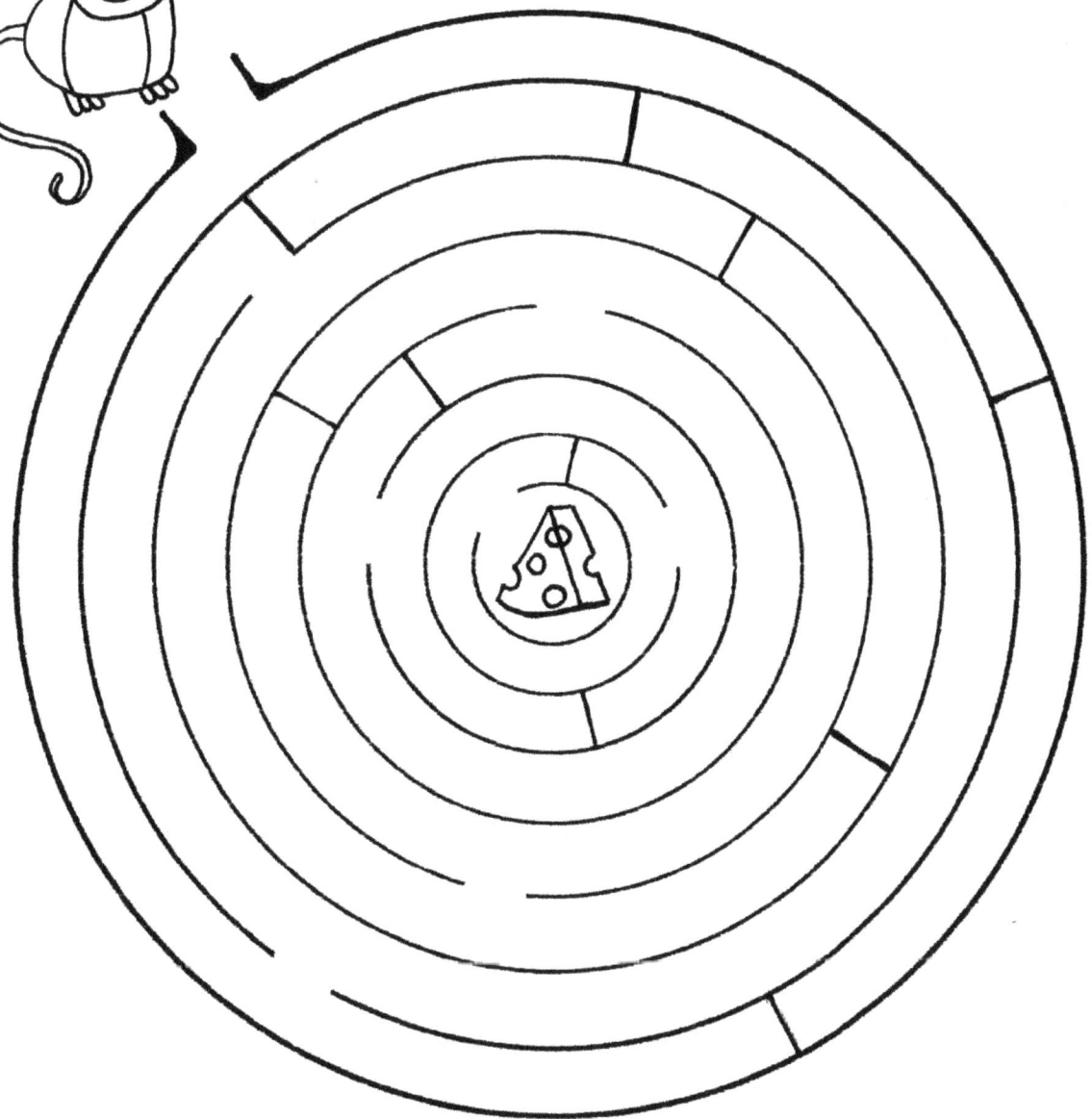

Print the words and draw a picture.

aaa

AAA

ape

ant

apple

Print the words and draw a picture.

bbb

BBB

bee

bat

boat

Print the words and
draw a picture.

c c c

c c c

cat

coat

camera

Print the words and draw a picture.

d d d

D D D

d o g

d i m e

d o n k e y

Print the words and draw a picture.

e e e

E E E

egg

eagle

elephant

Print the words. Draw the other half. Color it!

Bunny

Rabbit

Connect the dot, both letters and numbers. Then color in your surprise picture

 # TIC-TAC-TOE

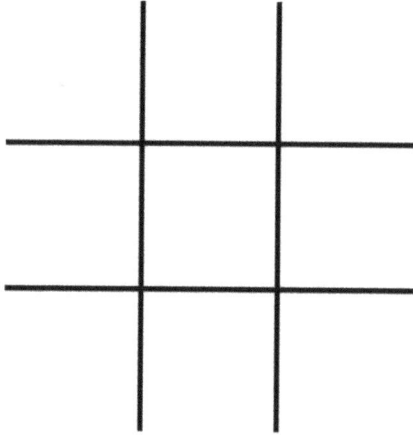 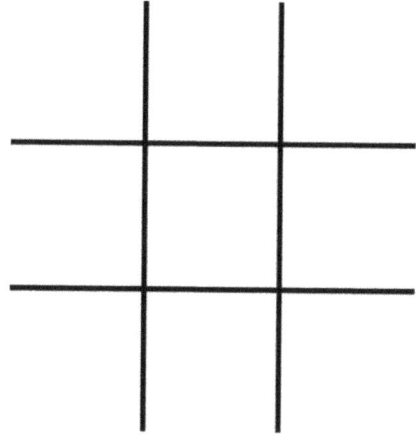

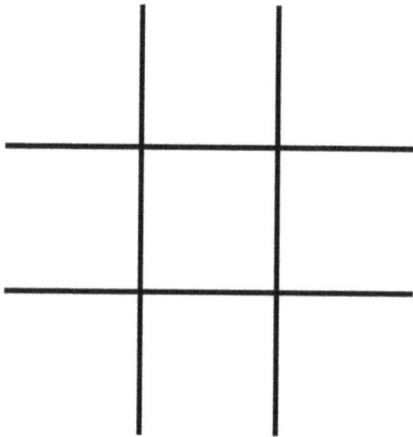 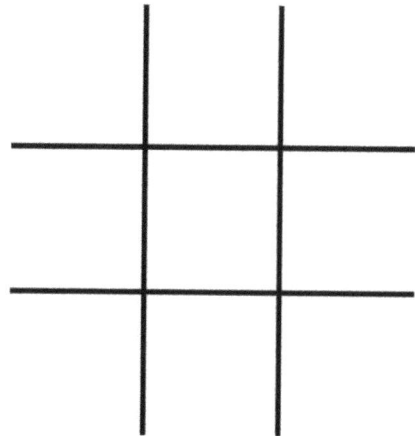

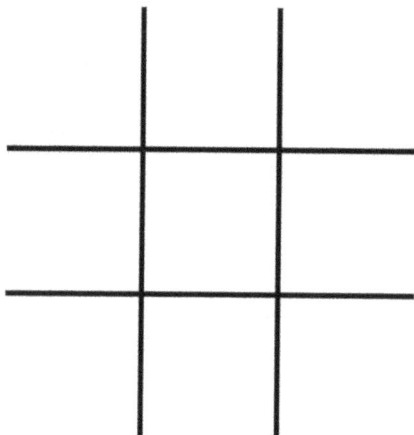 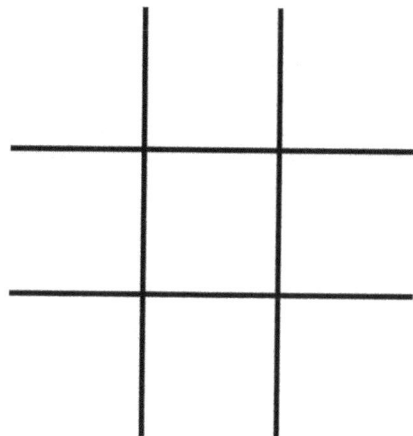

Print the words and draw a picture.

f f f

F F F

fun

fish

fairy

Print the words and draw a picture.

ggg

GGG

gab

goat

giant

Print the words and draw a picture.

hhh

HHH

hop

happy

horse

Print the words and draw a picture.

i i i

I I I

ice

igloo

island

Print the words and draw a picture.

jjj

JJJ

jam

jelly

jigsaw

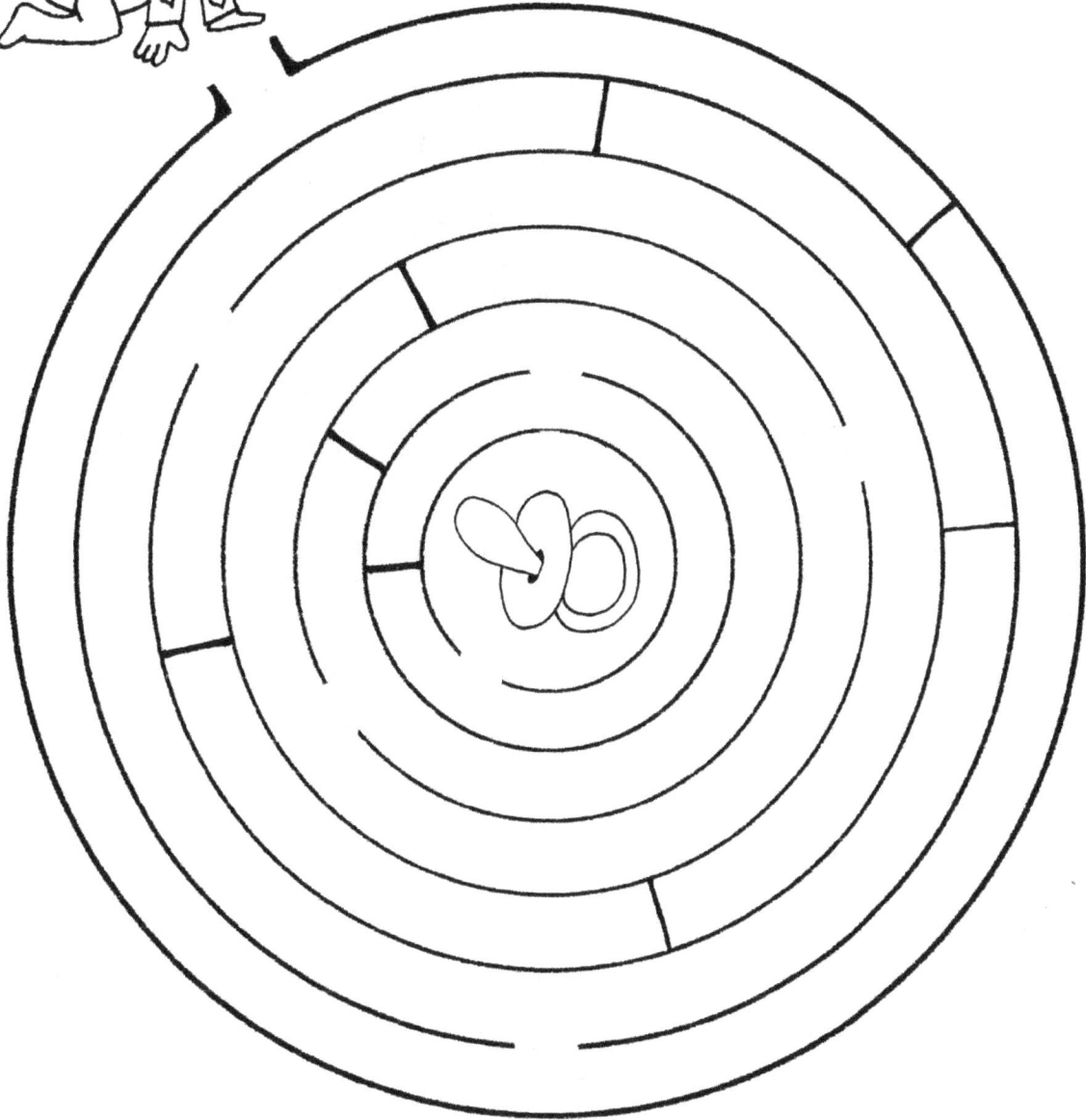

Print the words. Draw the other half. Color it!

Spring

Flowers

Print the words and draw a picture.

kkk

KKK

key

kite

kangaroo

Print the words and
draw a picture.

Ll

LLL

leg

lasso

leopard

Print the words and draw a picture.

mmm

MMM

mix

mouse

monkey

Print the words and draw a picture.

nnn

NNN

Nap

Nice

nickle

Print the words and draw a picture.

O O O

O O O

o w l

o i n k

o t t e r

Print the words. Draw the other half. Color it!

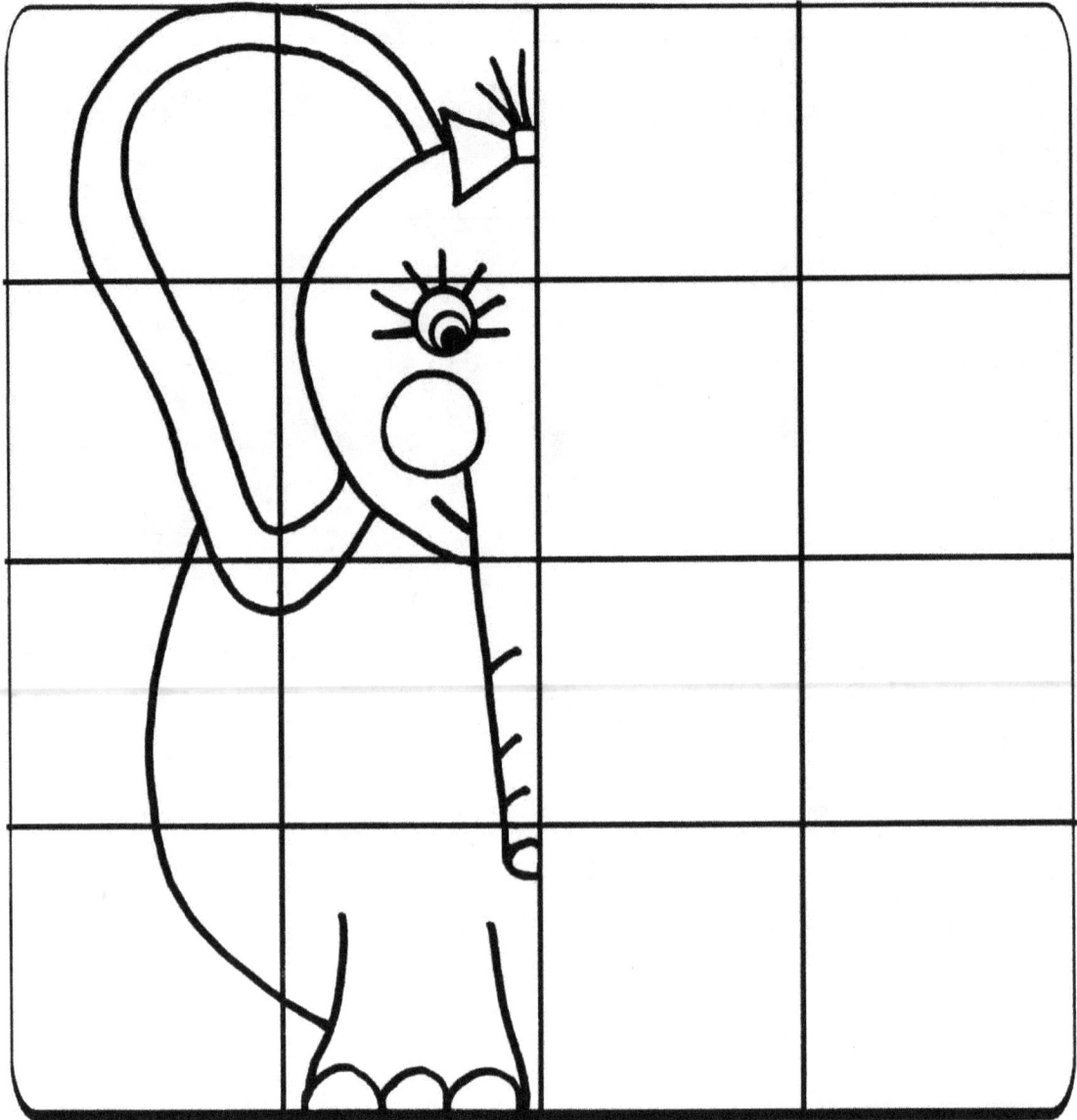

Lucky

Elephant

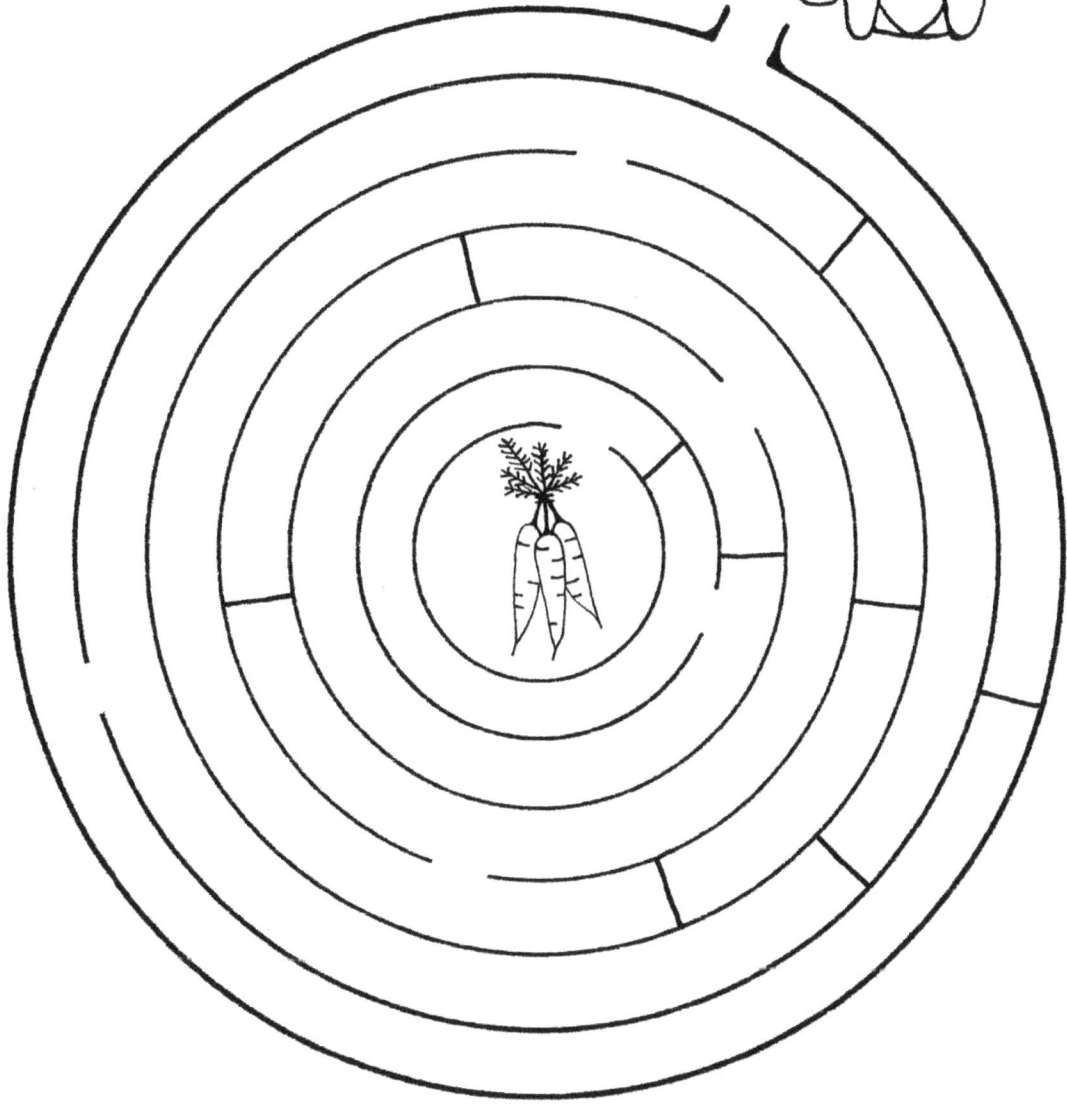

Print the words and draw a picture.

ppp

PPP

pig

pears

penguins

Print the words and draw a picture.

qqq

QQQ

quill

quick

queen

Print the words and draw a picture.

rrr

RRR

red

rabbit

rocket

Print the words and draw a picture.

sss

sss

sea

shoes

snakes

Print the words and draw a picture.

ttt

TTT

toes

tacos

turtle

Print the words. Draw the other half. Color it!

Space

People

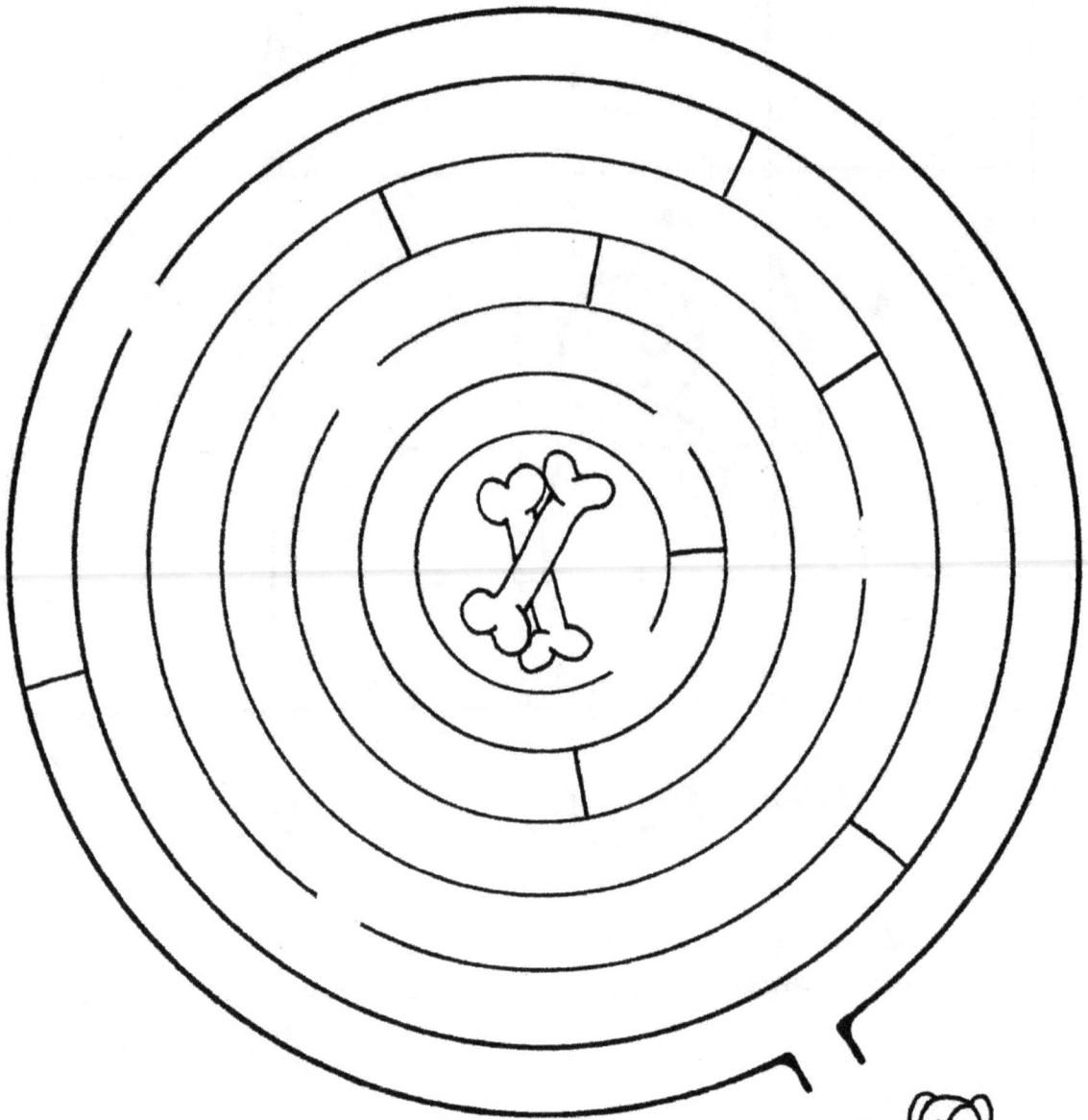

TIC-TAC-TOE

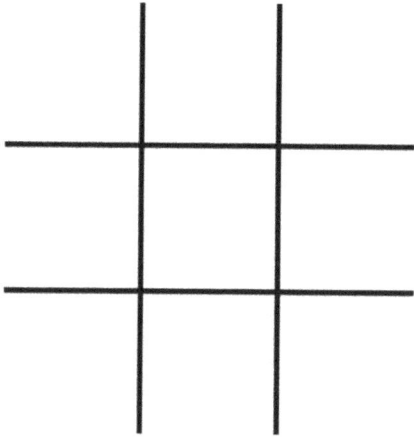
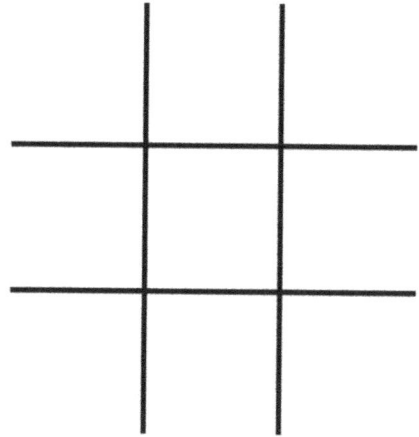
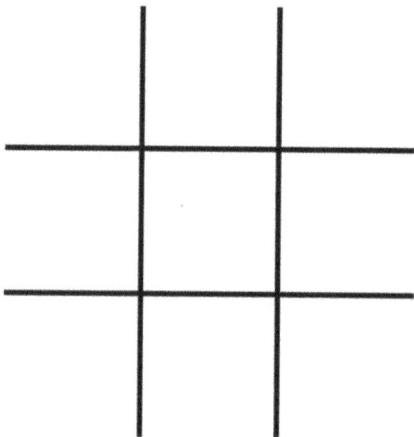
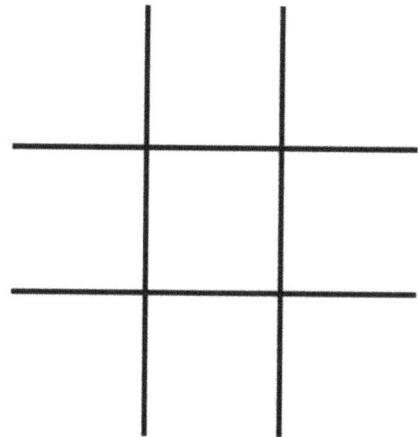
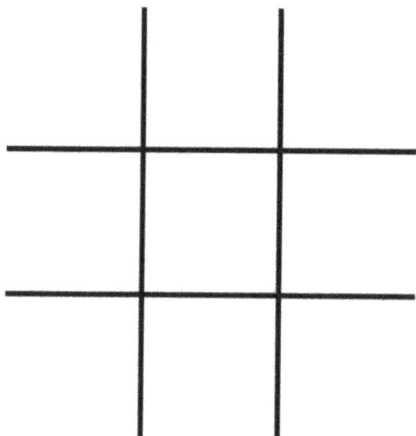
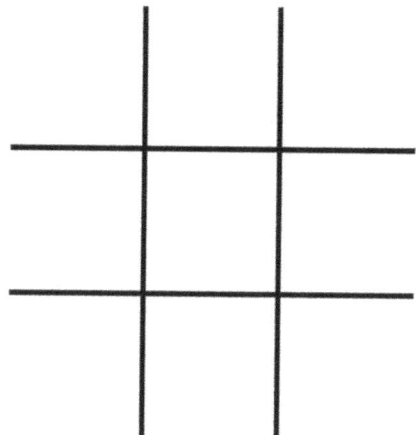

Connect the dot.
Then color in your
surprise picture

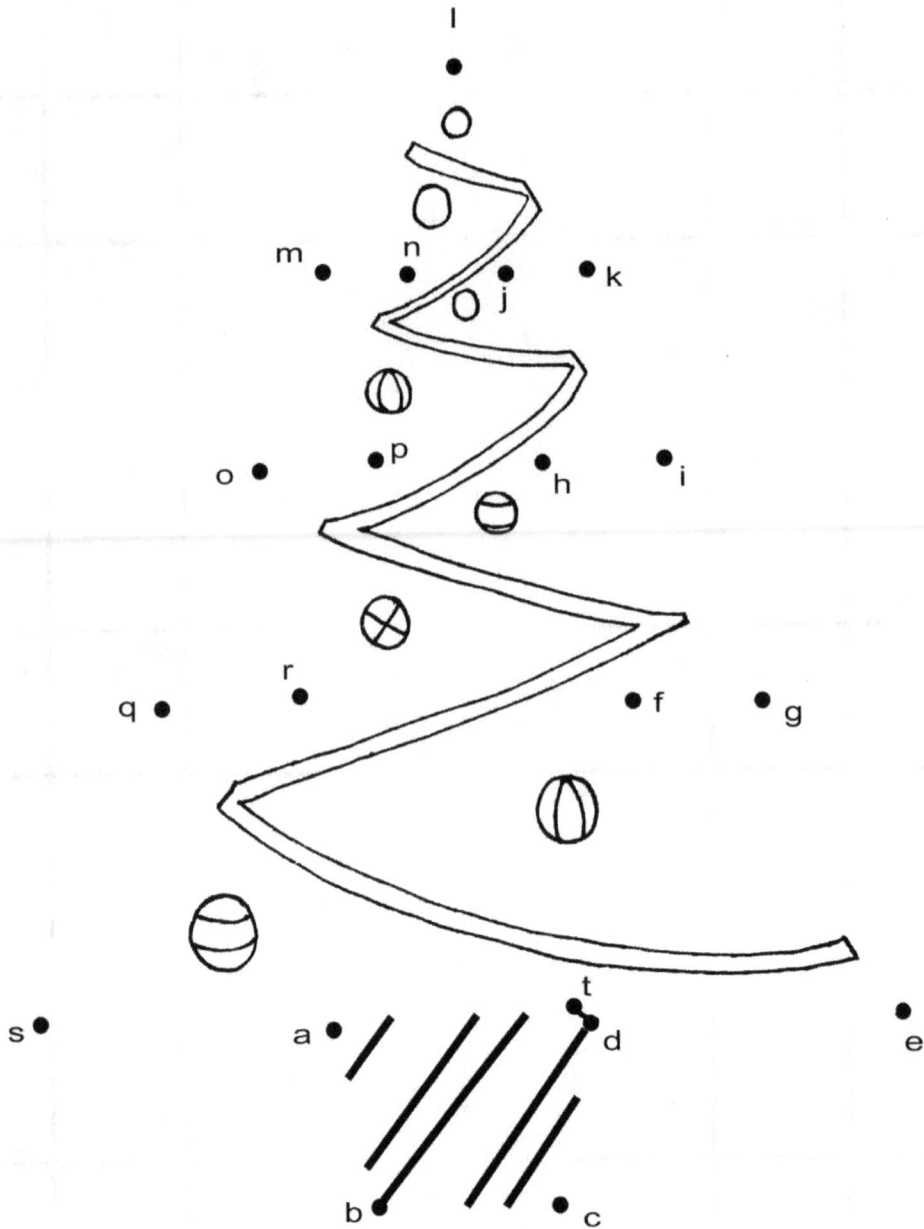

l

m   n   k
j

o   p   h   i

r
q   f   g

s   a   t   d   e

b   c

Print the words and draw a picture.

u u u

u u u

upper

uncle

unicorn

Print the words and draw a picture.

v v v

v v v

vest

violin

vegetables

Print the words and draw a picture.

w w w

w w w

walk

whale

waffle

Print the words and draw a picture.

x x x

x x x

x ray

xenon

xylophone

Print the words and draw a picture.

y y y

Y Y Y

yak

yarn

yokes

Print the words and draw a picture.

Z Z Z

Z Z Z

zipper

zebra

zigzag

Print the words. Draw the other half. Color it!

Silly

Lion

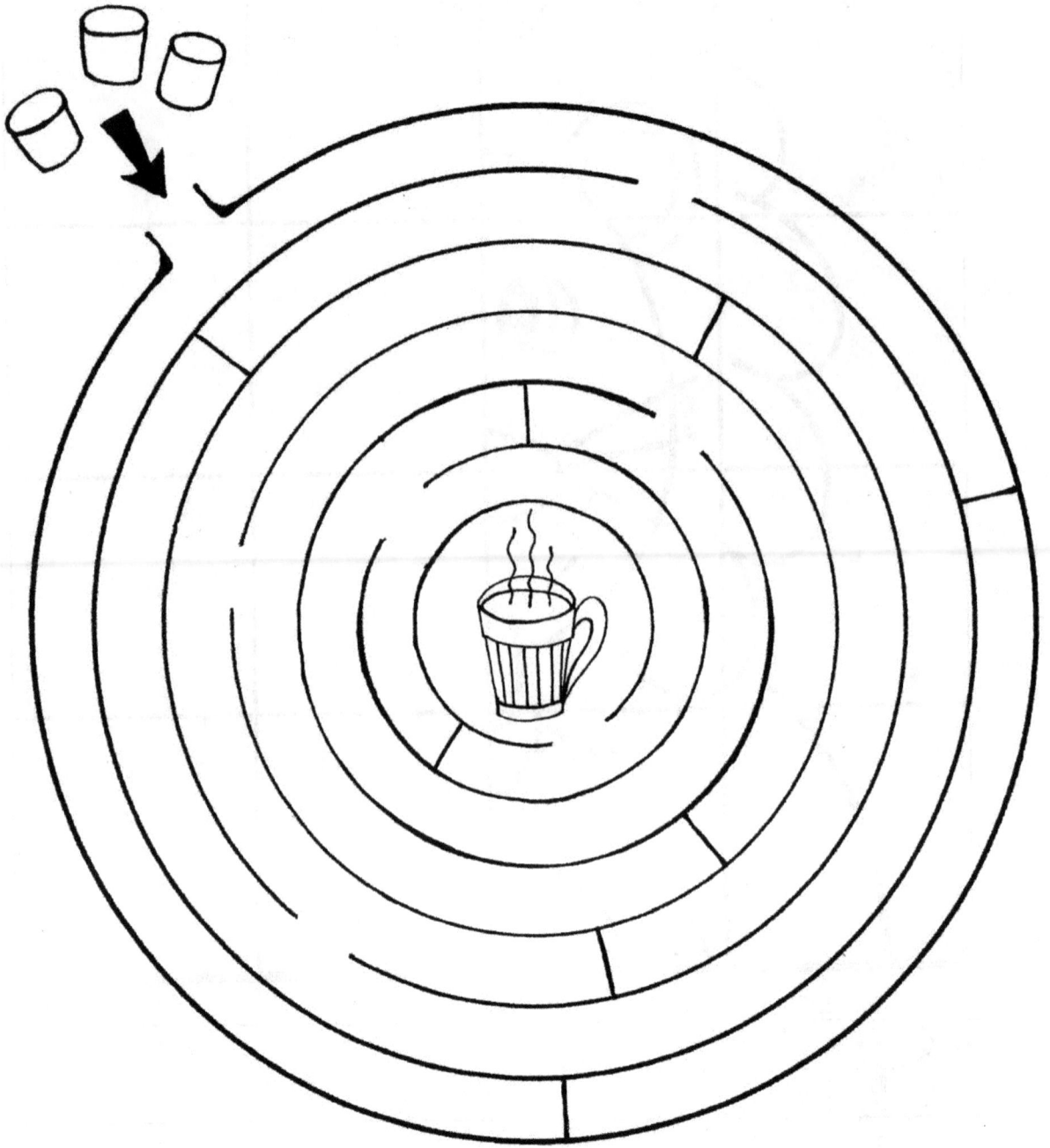

1 1 1

2 2 2

3 3 3

4 4 4

5 5 5

6 6 6

7 7 7

8 8 8

9 9 9

10 10 10

1 one

2 two

3 three

4 four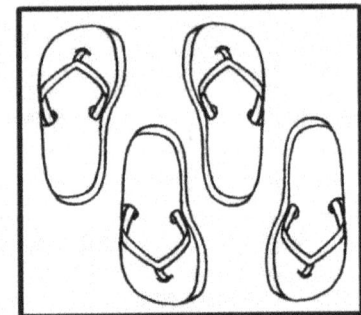

5 five

6   six

7   seven

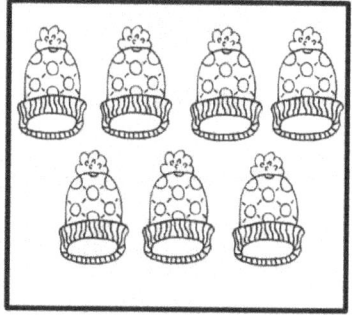

8   eight

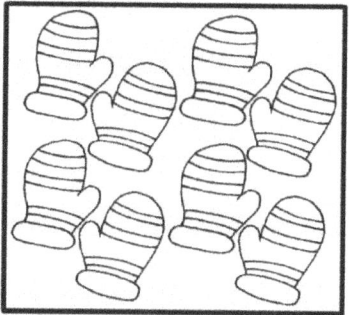

9   nine

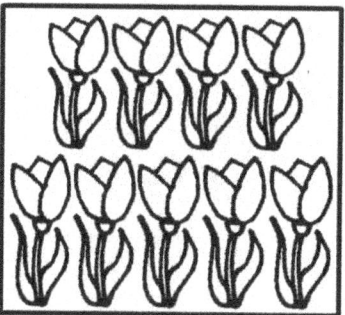

10   ten

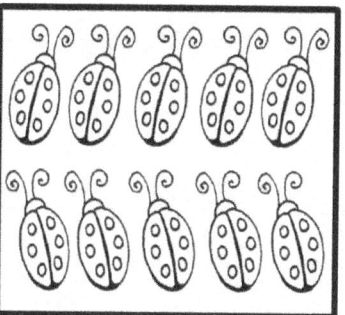

Circle the one that is different.

Count the number of things in each row.
Then circle the number that matches.

1 2 3 4 5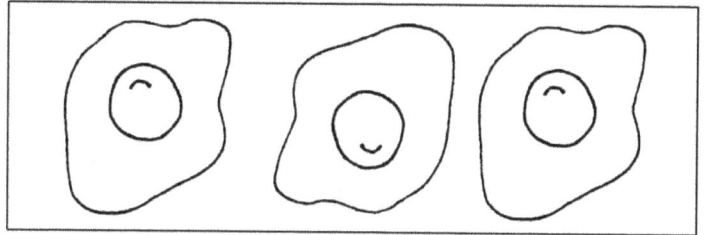

1 2 3 4 5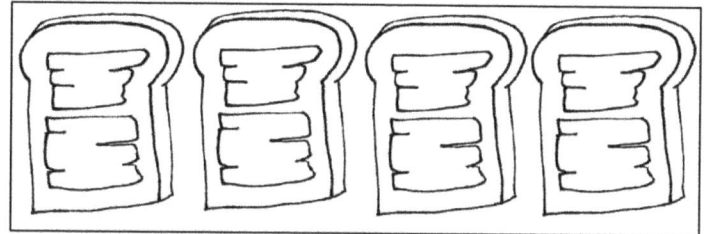

1 2 3 4 5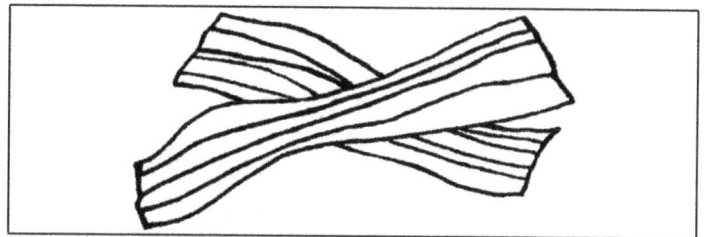

1 2 3 4 5

1 2 3 4 5

1 2 3 4 5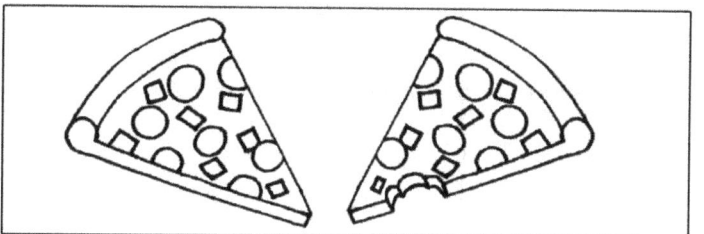

TIC-TAC-TOE

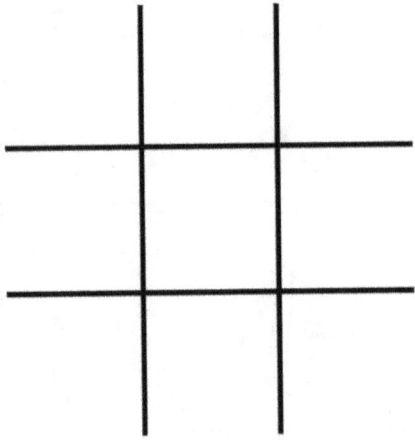
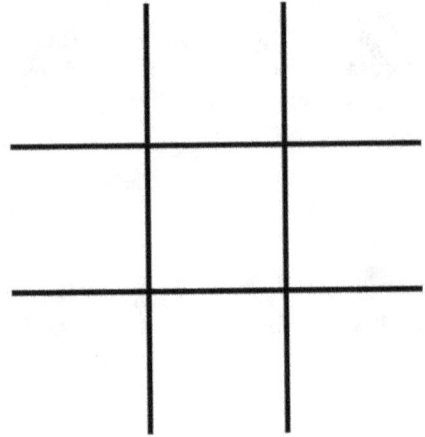
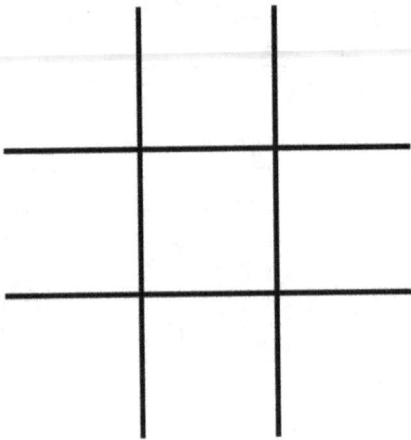
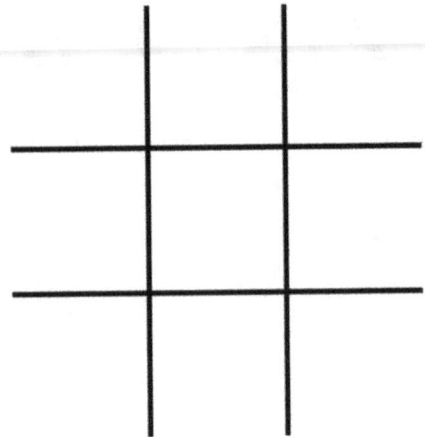
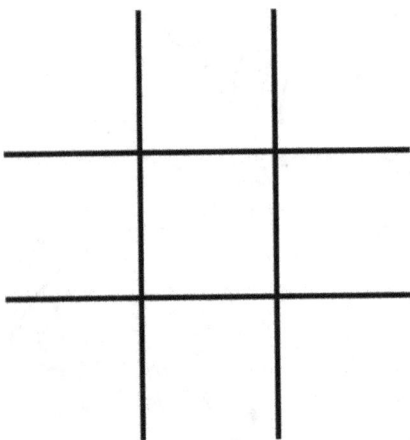
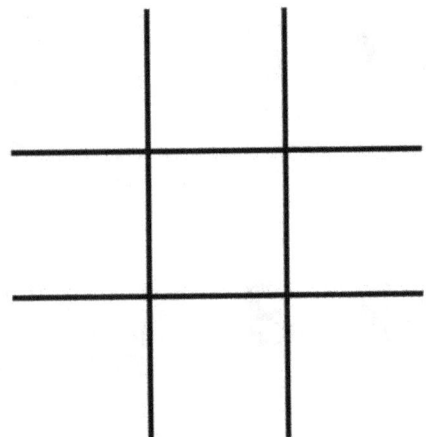

Count the number of things in each row.
Then circle the number that matches.

1 2 3 4 5

1 2 3 4 5

1 2 3 4 5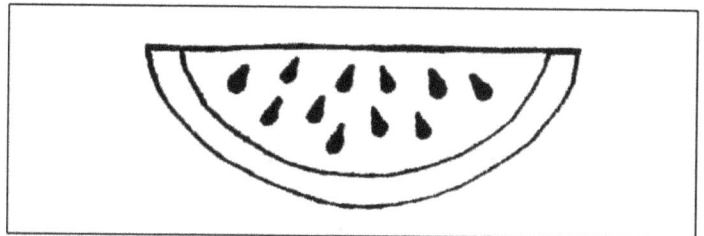

1 2 3 4 5

1 2 3 4 5

1 2 3 4 5

Connect the dots, both letters and numbers Then color in your surprise picture

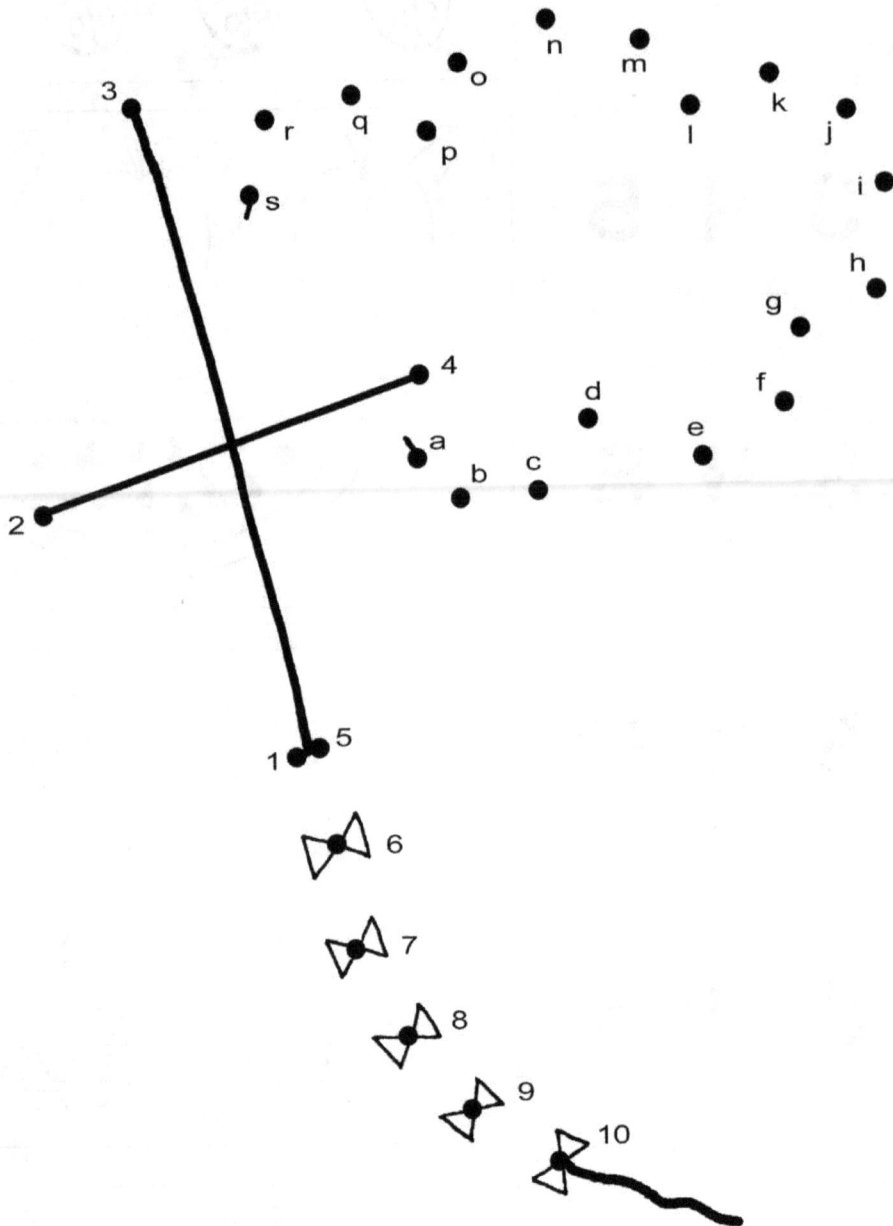

Circle the one that is different.

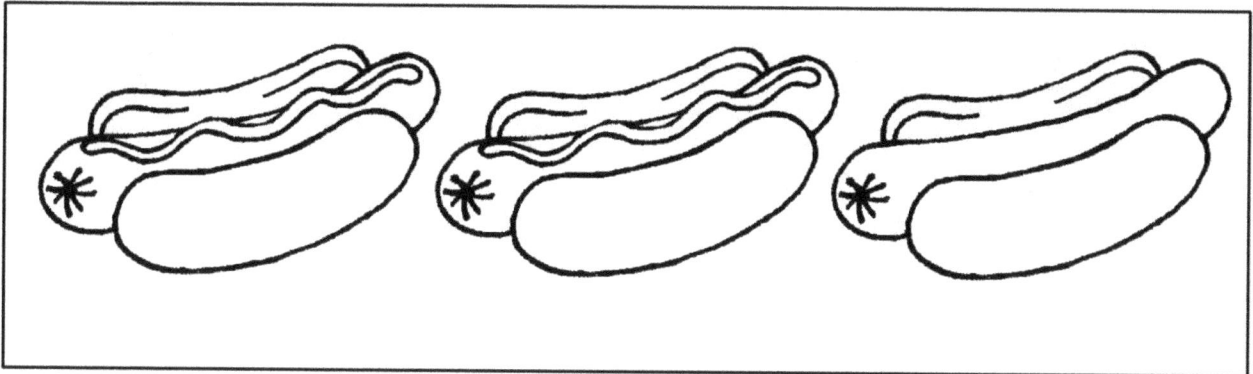

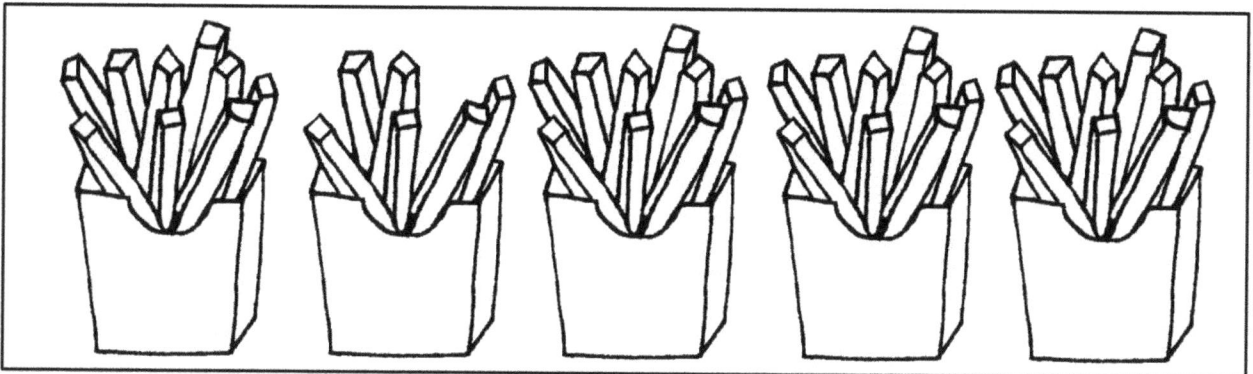

TIC-TAC-TOE

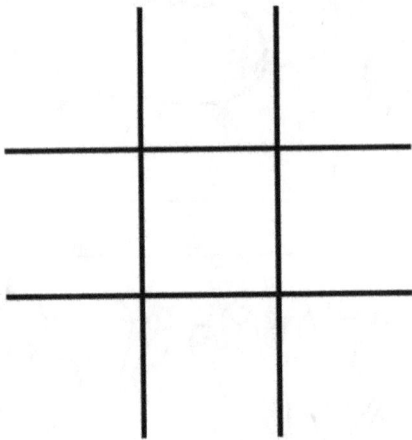
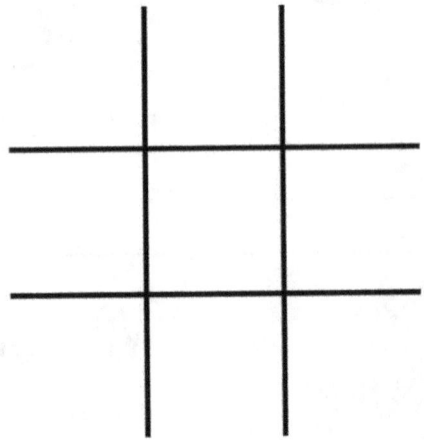
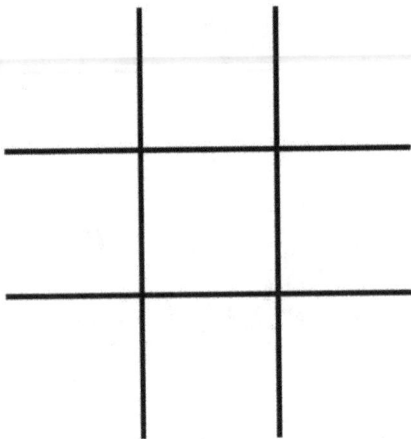
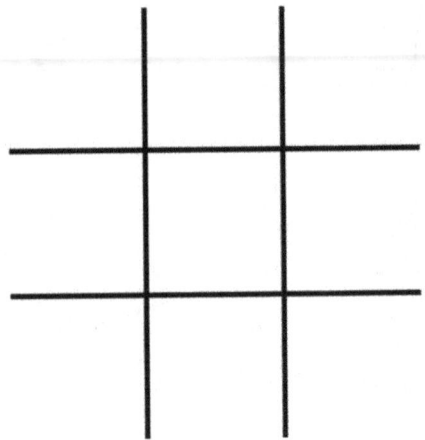
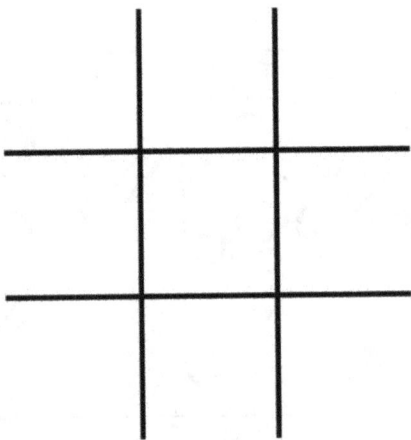
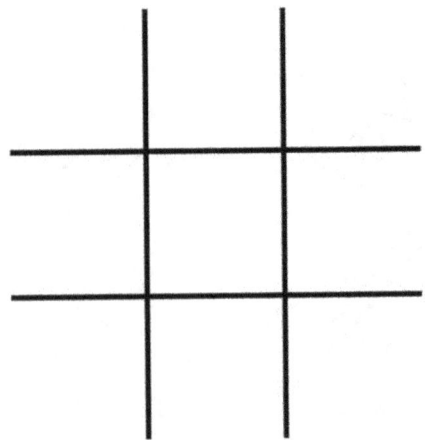

Count the number of things in each row.
Then circle the number that matches.

1 2 3 4 5

1 2 3 4 5

1 2 3 4 5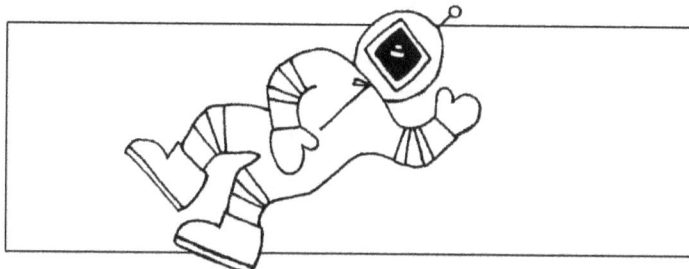

1 2 3 4 5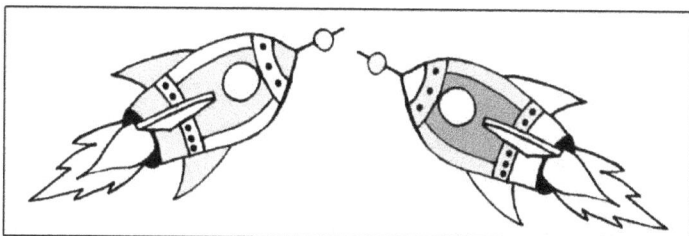

1 2 3 4 5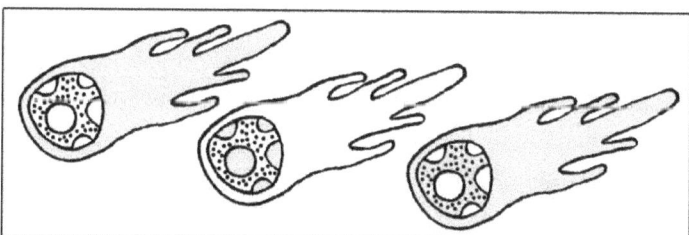

1 2 3 4 5

Circle the one that is different.

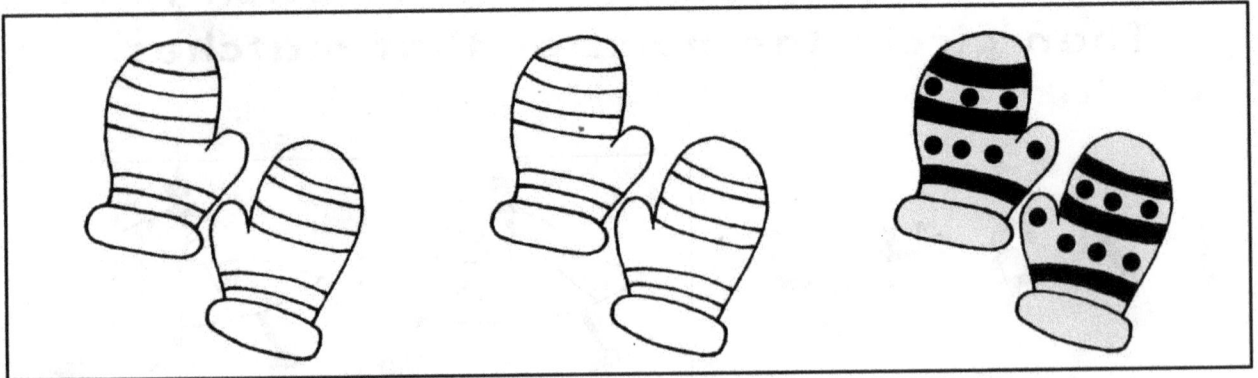

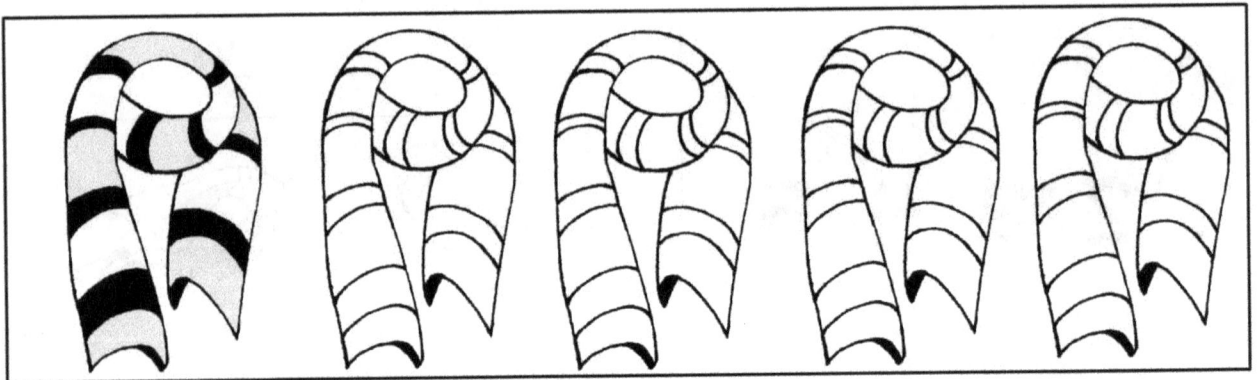

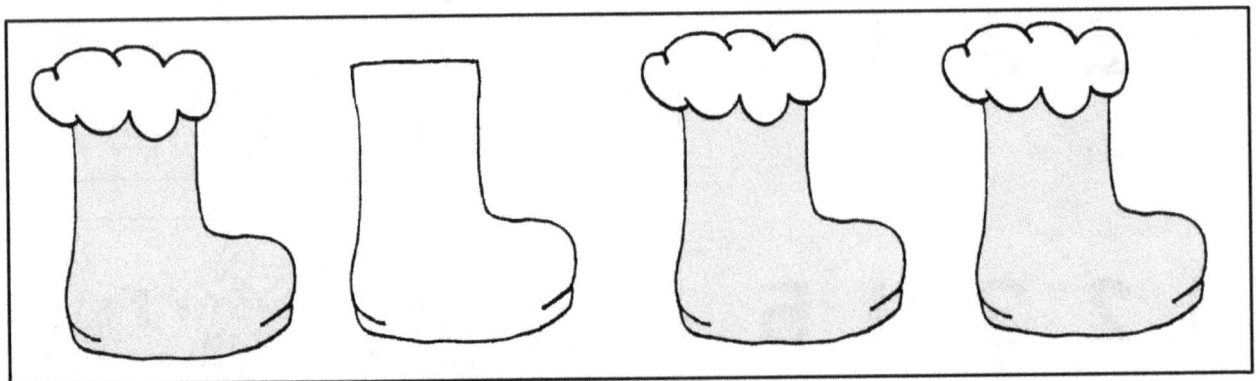

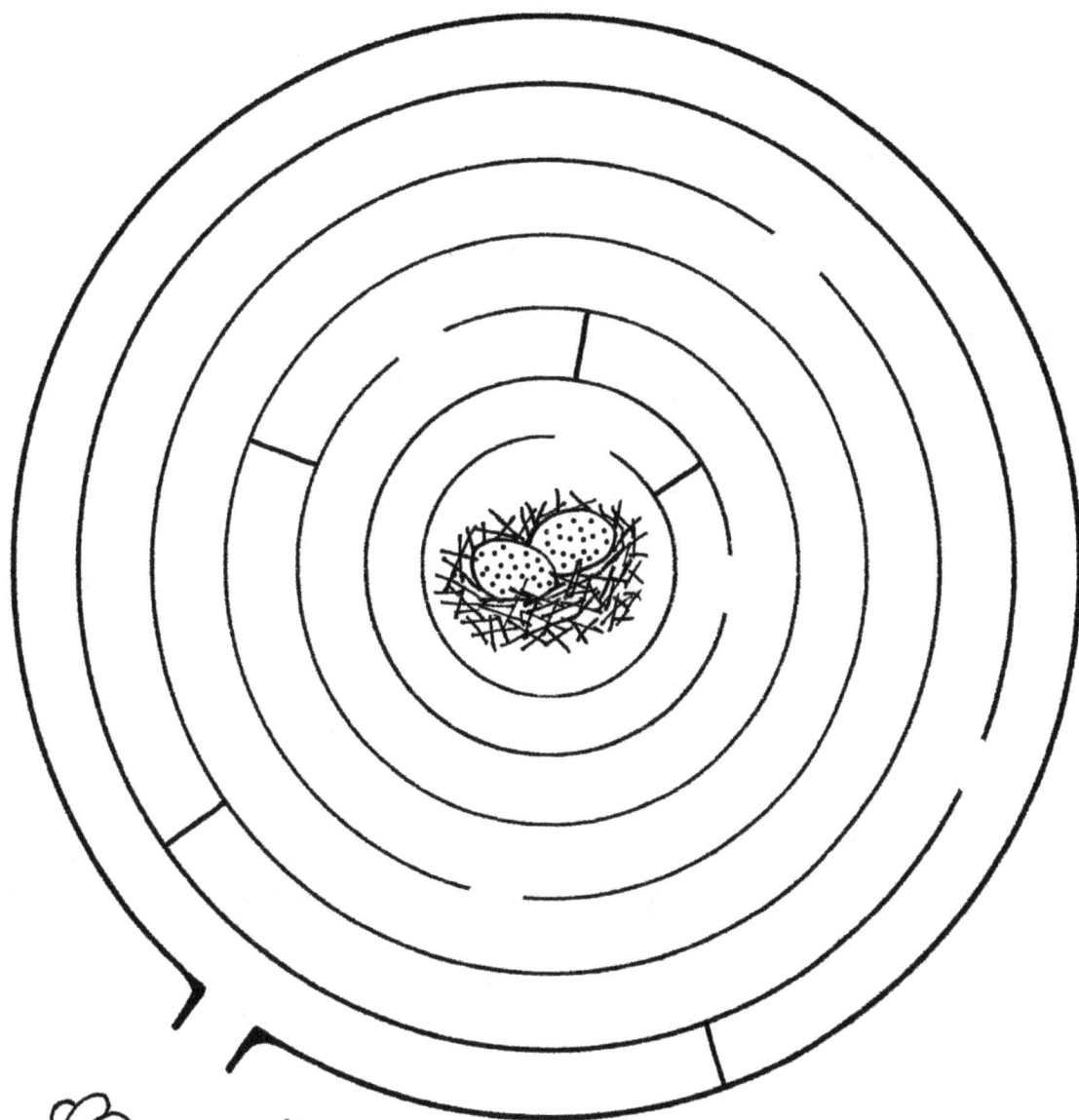

Circle the one that is different.

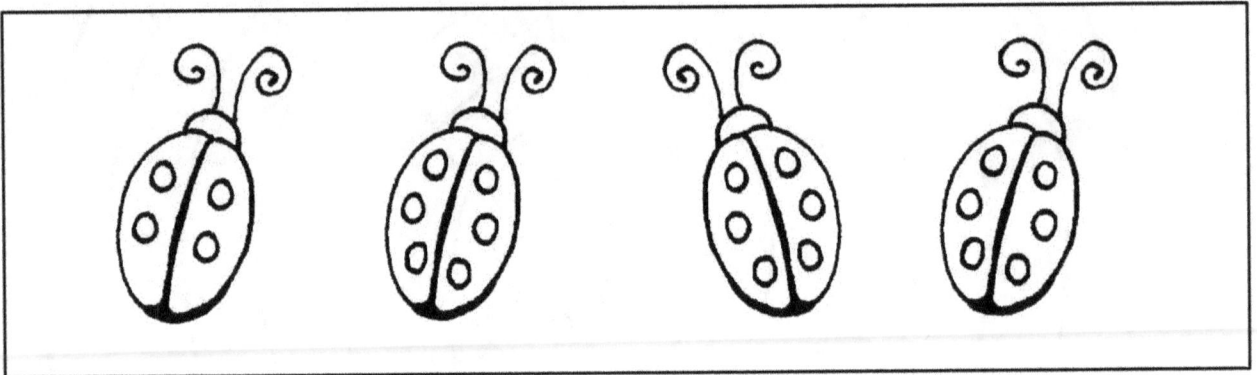

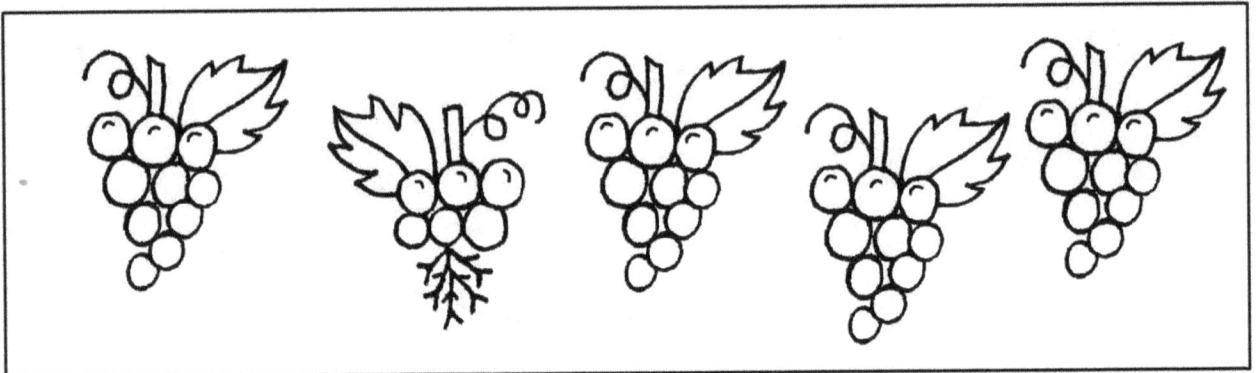

 # TIC-TAC-TOE

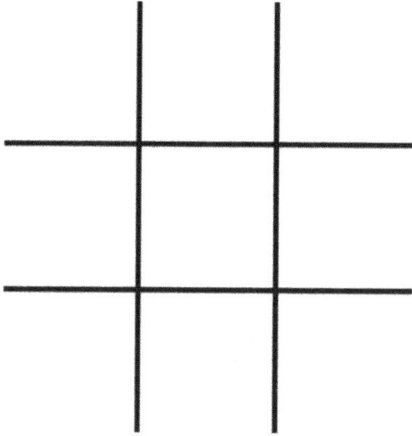

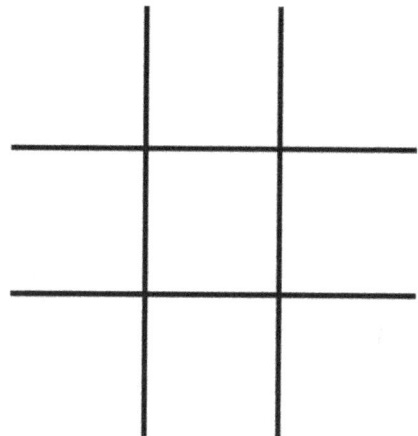

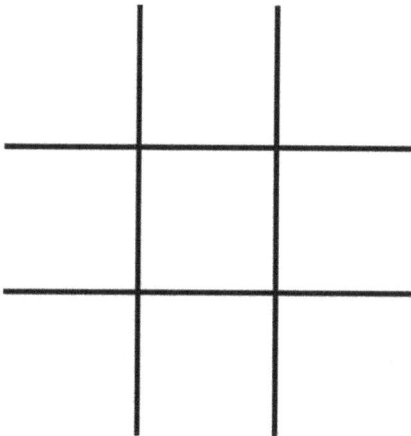

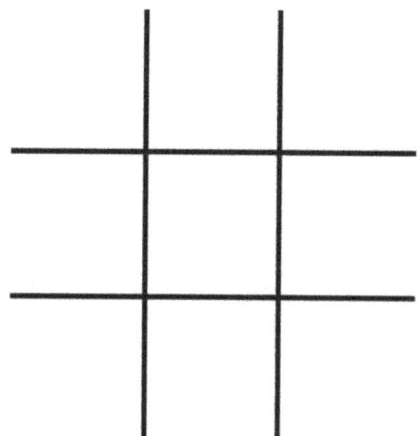

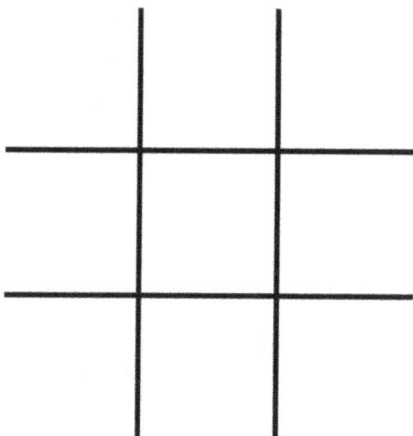

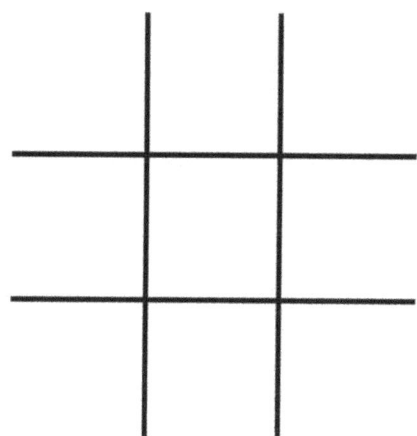

Count the number of things in each row.
Then circle the number that matches.

1 2 3 4 5

1 2 3 4 5

1 2 3 4 5

1 2 3 4 5

1 2 3 4 5

1 2 3 4 5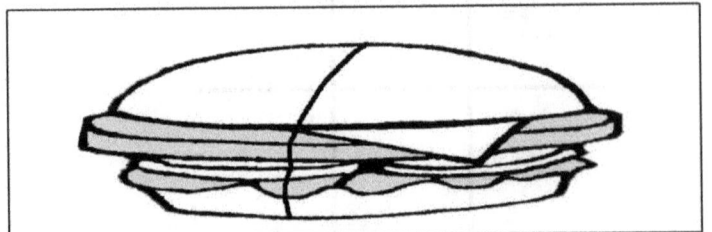

Connect the dots, both letters and numbers Then color in your surprise picture

Circle the one that is different.

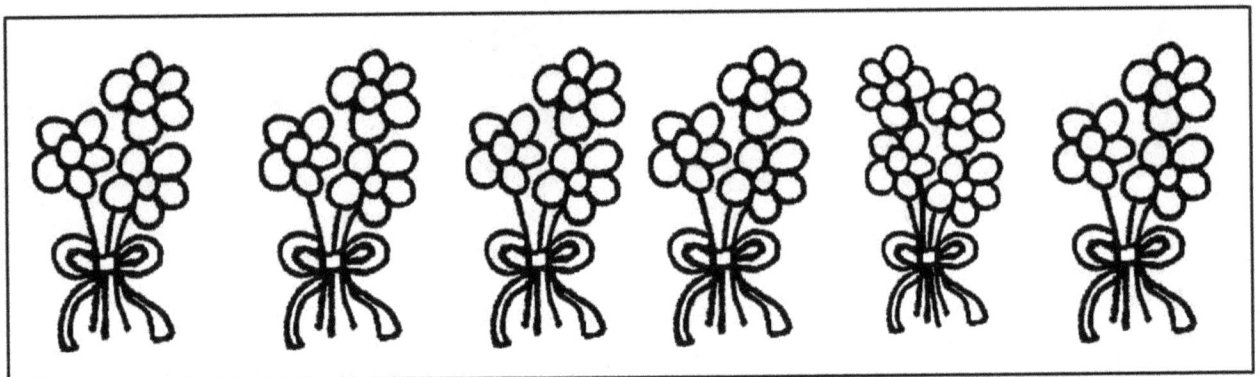

Has your child enjoyed this book?
Please leave me a review!
I would love to hear your feed back
Thank you for purchasing my product.
Your support is greatly appreciated.

www.ingramcontent.com/pod-product-compliance
Lightning Source LLC
Chambersburg PA
CBHW081637040426
42449CB00014B/3346